Dar

MW01245295

Travis DeLaney

BookLeaf Publishing

Darc Raven's Words © 2022 Travis DeLaney

All rights reserved.

Travis DeLaney asserts the moral right to be identified as author of this work.

Presentation by *BookLeaf Publishing*

Web: www.bookleafpub.com

E-mail: info@bookleafpub.com

ISBN: 978-93-5761-046-9

First edition 2022

PREFACE

"Long after I'm gone, they stick in the minds of others... my words" -Darc Raven (A.K.A. Travis DeLaney)

Honor the Fallen

There are many who have died...
But live in our memories...
They could at times get on our nearves
But they were loved anyways...
In life, they were family and friends...
In death, they are but gaps in our hearts...
Holes that can't be filled by anyone else...
Missing presences that can't be replaced...
You may or may not have known them,
You may have only heard of them...
It matters not... we, still, can all
Honor the Fallen

Nature's Storm Waltz

Cyclone
Movement, flow, rhythm
Power uncontrolled
Beautifully devastating
Nature's Storm Waltz
Gaia's Last Symphony
Unleashed

Divine Lips of Graceful Beauty

Destiny, so very captivating
Inviting beauty, enticing love
Vital to my heart and soul
I am engulfed with passions
Never thought existed
Enchanted, for always and ever

Love, so pure
Igniting my desire
Perfectly enthused
Satisfied by your presence

Opened, my life is
For you and you only

Glowing with elegance
Radiant and enchanting
Always dazzling
Completely robed in splendor
Entirely glimmering with beauty
Flattering in all your ways
Unmatchable in your grace
Laminating, the fires of your purity are

Beloved Angel, charming, are thee
Enthralled by your magnificence
Attracted from your very nature
Under a spell, one of love
Trapped forever and eternity
Yearning for thee

The Hunt

Moonlight down upon flesh
Glisten in the eyes
Scent of the prey enmesh
Within frosted skies

Shivers of the unexpecting
Grazing in a nearby grove
Ears do perk with alerting
As sounds, to fear, had drove

Darting, Dashing, this way and that
Running frantically on the sense of danger
Unaware, quick and blind as a bat
Bolts far away, much fear of the stranger

Finding itself trapped, cornered, lost
Sounds turn to growls in the night
Throat gripped suddenly and is then tossed
The hunter sparing it's prey none of its might

Emerging into light, the prey does land
Fear on it's face, the face of a man
Thuds and growls, footprints in the sand
Eyes and fangs stepping forth, a lycan

The man knowing this day, his doom
Rain starts to fall as if the sky were aware
With the flash of lightning and a thunderous
boom
The sounds of screaming silenced with rip and
tear

Moments later all is still
The corpus lay cold
The beast satisfied with the taste of it's kill
Another death to add to the story of old

A kiss

I lay alone at night
Cold, wet, scared, depressed
Wishing to leave this world
Laying there, someone came
A beautiful and majestic woman
Exquisite in her stride
Gracefully, she spoke to me
Stood at her bidding, we strolled.
Hours upon hours we walked
Time faded away as we talked
Only her and I was I aware of
Her splendor, intoxicating
Her elegance, perfect in it's scent
Her presence, warmed my cold heart
I became infatuated, obsessed with her
She, in turn, seemed to have fallen for me.
To her, I told that if I were to die
In her arms is where I'd wish my last breaths
She smiled and pulled me in close
Smiling in return, for my life seemed good
Leaning in to her as she leaned into me.

A kiss, a simple kiss
Looking into her eyes as they hollowed out
Frightened once again
Then knowledge revealed and peace came to me
As I lay lifeless in her arms.
All from a simple kiss
A kiss from Death

Rebirth

Thoughts
Wondering ideas
Never ceasing
Never revealing

Open my eyes
Show me what lies within
Let understanding invade my mind
Acknowledgement is what I need

Thoughts
Burning me with wondering
Let me comprehend
Let the curiosity end

My mind is ajar
For knowledge that I seek
Teach me what I don't know
Let me learn and absorb ideas

My mind, expanding
My thoughts, transforming
My ideas reconfiguring
Myself, altering

Rebirth through new insight

Monster

Monster

Stalking prey within the night
The scent of blood thick as smog
Silent screams ring in the deaf ears of the fallen

How should I feel?

When the darkness surrounds me
Gripping me tightly
Pulling at the lifeless husks

Creatures lie here

My soul blackened and exposed
Bloodlust and madness wrapped together
I peer down upon those death embraces

Looking through the window

My eyes show the lack of regret
The twisted smile upon my lips
Reveals my truth once hidden

Monster

Love of an Elegant Maiden

Lonely without thee
Only longing
Vigorously waiting
Ever for thee

Oh what bliss it is
For me to have you by me

Afraid of losing thee
Nearly had lost once

Eternally yours to love
Limitless adoration back to thee
Enchant me with an endless waltz
Grace me with your perfection
And immortal passions shall be yours
Now and forever, the fires of my heart will burn
The blaze of my spirit for thee

My life, fuller from you
An enchanting elegance
In marveled by your essence
Divine, as it is
Enticed my soul
Never wanting to let go

Sunrise (Sky)

Shimmering open
Kaleidoscope of colors
Yields not to darkness

The Demons Feast

The demons within the heart
Poisoning the mind
Has been from the start
Pain becomes designed

Poisoning the mind
Perverting what is real
Pain becomes designed
Suffering, what a meal

Perverting what is real
Confusion sown by the hour
Suffering, what a meal
Pain, the demons' devour

Confusion sown by the hour
Has been from the start
Pain, the demons' devour
The demons within the heart

Sparkling Angel

Sparkling Angel,
My love and my savior
Oh, how my eyes were shut
My ears deafened by sweet words
Words from your mouth

(Lies and deceit...
Dreams that I wished to be true
The smile when you tore me apart
I remember them all)

Sparkling Angel,
How the darkness bleeds from you
The emotions and feelings for me
Happiness personified
Glittering eyes upon your sight

(Lies and deceit...
Dreams that I wished to be true
The smile when you tore me apart
I remember them all)

Fallen Angel,
What is the reason?
The knife in my back
The world betrayed you,
But never did my love.

(Lies and deceit...
Dreams that I wished to be true
The smile when you tore me apart
I remember them all)

We could have lasted
Should have held on tightly
What would have become of us then?
We will never know now
For now we have reached an end.

(Lies and deceit...
Dreams that I wished to be true
The smile when you tore me apart
I remember them all)

Roses from heaven
(Rain/Rise)

Roses from heaven, fall
Around the lifeless void
Incarcerated souls lost within
Never to live once more

(Rain)
Falling, the showers of beauty
Each holds sparks of life
The empty forms of once man
Departed spirits entraped
Within roses from heaven
(Rise...)

Return to heaven, the roses
Into the sky from whence they came
Souls bound to beauties from above
Entering the gates, passed unto death

(...Rise)
Into the skys, they do return
Containers for souls,
Roses from heaven

Love and the Pain of Lies

Love, to have love
Great in all its glory
Blinding in its splendor
Opening for lies to lay within

Deceit, falsehoods

Fabrications pulled over your eyes
A light that shines bright enough to blind you
Till the darkness crushes you
And the truth is known

Destroyed, falling apart

To watch your life, your world crumble
Knowing that the one you loved and trusted
The one you thought cared
Was the cause of your demise

Magical, mystical

Your relationship once was
Thoughts of the past race through your head
As you fall from the highs you were in
Plummeting, quickly, towards the ground

Death, the final rest

A release better then this fate
The fate as the fine glass around your heart
Touch by truth, shattered by reality
Destroying what once was pure beauty

Bleeding, never healing

The glass that was your love
Remaining shattered
Leaving your heart tattered
Scared for eternity

From Love and the Pain of Lies

Silence now and forever

It starts with...

Why did this happen
The loss of something true
Pain seeping within
Blades slicing through

... Love that then transforms...

It was so real
The love and desire
An angel so true
The passion of fire

... To pain and sorrow,

Broken wings turned to dust
I crashed down to this earth
Torn and bleeding to the end
through love, death had birth

Silence now and forever.

The only true forever
Darkness everlasting
Into the evernal night
my soul is casting

Open wounds

The holes, the vacant wounds
The pain that blooms
Nothing is as it seems
Nothing redeems
Hold me in
Let me bleed in sin
Burn my soul with open scars
Destroy me with falling stars
These wounds will never heal
For if they did, they would steal
The memories of my mistakes
And all other things that are the stakes
In this game of life
Played with words and a knife
To what end is this?
Why does this life exist?
Did my sorrow
Burrow
Deep into my heart
Or was it there from the start
Crawling in my skin
Making me breathe thin
Crumble me from inside
For the pain that hasn't lied
Burn

In turn
Everything I am
All but a scam
Empty holes
My former life holds
For nothing is as it seems
And the pain deems
That I bleed as I kneel
For these wounds will never heal

Breath

Breath into me, oh love
My lungs desire your breath
Make my soul and body
Live only for thee
All that I am, forever yours
The air within my lungs
Is but the air you breath into me
For it is you that sustains me
It is you that causes me to live
Myself only for thee, endlessly

Take my life into you
Never my own self, but you alone
Don't let me escape thy love
Take my breath away
And give me yours instead
Sustain me, so that I am yours alone
Your breath is the air I long to breath
Only and forever, always my love.

Over

Walls and fortresses fade away forever
Blood spilled slowly decays into the depths
Life loses meaning and dies
So what is left for me now

Safe with you, I was
Held high by your love
Walls protected me from pain
Fortresses brought me peace

My heart now drips with cold blood
My soul, buried in the debris of the walls
Nothing left of what once was
Never rebuilding, never healing

You, who betrayed my love for thee
Taking a knife and stabbing me
Never will forgiveness truly be yours
My heart will be whole nevermore

My world crumbled that day
Watching you go astray
From the love I had for you
And saying that we were through

Rebirthing Now

As the day moves on
And I fall within
I see my life crash
From the waves of sin
A rut of hollow lust
The will to take from one
What is not mine in just
To my heart's sorrow

Sick of the pain
Frustrated from shame
Needing to not be so lame
Before I go insane

Breaking the habits
Free from my chains
Changing all the bits
Forgotten all blames
Given a goal
A reason for it all
To make my life whole
Rebirthing now

Everything Falls

Rain falls
I sit and watch
Remembering our past
Wanting to cry

Tears fall
Sorrow fills my heart
The day I lost you
How it effects me so

Strength falls
As I become weak
I suffer so much
I can't take it anymore

Blood falls
My life comes to a close
My soul cries out
As it leaves my body

I fall
Down upon the ground
Nothing left
Not even pain

Everything falls
This is how it ends
I am released from this curse
Now that I'm dead

As I Lay Me Down to Sleep

As I lay me down to sleep
I watch my soul slip into the deep
Knowing that you sent me there
And that to drag you with is only fair
Life's not fair they said to me
Why that is I can not see
So as I lay me down to sleep
I let my soul slip into the deep

Never Again, Your Transgressions

My pain, my brokenness
Suffering from your sin against me
Bleeding in desperation
Dying emotionally

Never again!

Your sorrow, hidden well
Blinded by your shameful silence
Deaf to your heart's cry

Never again!

Nothing as it seems
Unable to see behind the wall
Kneeling... Bleeding...
Unable to heal myself

Your Transgressions...

Buried me
Tormented my heart
Destroyed my soul

Your Transgressions...

Brought you to your knees
And then back to me
For nothing was as it seemed

So now I say:
Never Again held against you,
Shall Your Transgressions be

Printed in the USA
CPSIA information can be obtained
at www.ICGtesting.com
LVHW020256250923
759083LV00017B/704

9 789357 610469